The Medium and the Message

Media Richness Theory Explained

Freudian Trips

Copyright Page

© 2024 by Freudian Trips

This book is a work of non-fiction. Unless otherwise noted, the author and the publisher make no explicit guarantees as to the accuracy of the information contained in this book and will not be held responsible for any errors or omissions.

Published by Omniterra Media Inc

First Edition

Visit the author's website at www.freudiantrips.com

Disclaimer

The views and opinions expressed in this book are those of the author(s) and do not necessarily reflect the official policy or position of any other agency, organization, employer, or company. The contents of this book are for informational and educational purposes only and are not intended to serve as professional advice, diagnosis, or treatment.

The information provided in this book is believed to be accurate and reliable as of the date of publication. However, it may include some errors or inaccuracies, and no warranty or guarantee is provided regarding the accuracy, timeliness, or applicability of the content.

Readers are encouraged to consult with professional philosophers, educators, or other qualified professionals where appropriate for personalized advice. The author(s) and publisher shall not be liable for any loss, damage, or harm caused or alleged to be caused, directly or indirectly, by the information or ideas contained, suggested, or referenced in this book.

By reading this book, the reader acknowledges and agrees that they are solely responsible for how they interpret and apply the information contained herein.

This book may also include references to other works, studies, and sources. These references are provided for further reading and exploration and do not imply endorsement or validation of the specific theories, viewpoints, or interpretations presented in those works.

Introduction: Does the Way We Talk Really Matter?

Think back to the last time you had a really important conversation. Maybe it was about a project at work, a decision with your family, or something big that happened with a friend. How did you have that conversation? Was it a face-to-face chat, a phone call, a chain of emails, or even a bunch of text messages?

Believe it or not, the way you choose to communicate can seriously impact how well things go. Two researchers, named Daft and Lengel, came up with something called Media Richness Theory (MRT for short). This theory helps us understand just how much the type of communication we use really, really matters.

The Ever-Changing World of Talking

Remember when phones were attached to walls, and the only way to "see" who you were talking to was in your imagination? Now, we have video calls literally in our pockets! Technology has exploded, giving us tons of ways to communicate: email, instant messaging, social media, video conferencing, the list goes on! But does this flood of options make things simpler...or more confusing?

Media Richness Theory helps us decide which communication tool is best for what job. Think about it: work, friendships, and even getting quick information are all very different situations. MRT helps us untangle the best ways to connect for each one.

Why This Book Matters

The whole purpose of this book is to dive into Media Richness Theory and make it understandable. We'll look at how to choose the right way to communicate depending on whether your message is simple or super complicated. Misunderstandings happen, right? MRT can help us cut back on those!

Here's a Taste of What's to Come...

Imagine you're starting a new project at work. Simple emails might be okay for basic updates, but what about tackling a big problem together? That might be better with a video chat where you can share ideas quickly and even see each other's reactions. On the flip side, sending a heartfelt, personal message to a friend probably works a lot better in a handwritten note than a quick text they might misinterpret.

These are just little examples. We're going to get into all the exciting reasons why the medium you choose (email, text, voice, video, etc.) heavily influences the message you send.

Chapter 1: Not All Communication Is Created Equal

Let's play a game! Imagine you need to teach a friend how to tie a fancy knot. Here are your options:

- **Option 1:** Write out instructions in an email.
- **Option 2:** Call them on the phone and explain the steps.
- **Option 3:** Meet up and show them how with a real rope.

Which option would be easiest for your friend to understand? Most people would say Option 3–showing them in person! Why? Because you can see each other's faces, use your hands, and adjust your teaching if they seem confused.

This is the heart of Media Richness Theory. It's all about realizing that different ways of communicating are better for different tasks. Let's break it down:

The Richness Scale

Think of communication like a scale. At one end, you have "lean" communication. This is like sending a quick text or a basic email–there's not much room for detail or instant feedback. At the other end is super "rich" communication, like a face-to-face conversation. This is packed with all sorts of info: the speaker's tone of voice, their facial expressions, and more.

What Makes a Message "Rich"?

Here's where it gets interesting:

- **Instant Feedback:** Can you get a quick response and have a back-and-forth? Rich communication is like a lively tennis match, while lean communication is more like leaving someone a voicemail.
- **All the Cues:** Imagine trying to explain emotions over text. Tricky, right? Rich communication has those extra elements: body language, tone of voice, eye contact...all the things that make messages crystal clear.
- **Language Variety:** Rich communication lets you explain things fully, using the right words for the situation. It's the difference between a simple "good job!" text and a thoughtful, in-person word of praise.
- **That Personal Touch:** A handwritten card feels way more special than a mass email, doesn't it? Rich communication lets you add personality and warmth that can easily get lost in a text.

Why Does This Matter?

Choosing the right communication "tool" is like having the right tool for a DIY project. You wouldn't use a hammer to fix a leaky pipe, right? The same goes for communication: using a text message to solve a complex work problem is probably going to lead to frustration!

I hope this chapter makes the idea of "media richness" a little clearer. Think of it as your guide to picking the best way to communicate for every situation!

Chapter 2: Cutting Through the Confusion

Imagine you're listening to directions, but they sound like a jumbled mess. Or maybe you read a text message from a friend and have zero clue if they're happy, sad, or joking. Ugh, frustrating, right? This is where the ideas of "uncertainty" and "equivocality" come in.

- **Uncertainty:** This is basically when you lack information. Like if your boss sends a vague email about a project, leaving you with more questions than answers.
- **Equivocality:** Think of this as having too many possible meanings. Is that text from your friend sarcastic or sincere? Was that raised eyebrow from your coworker a sign of interest or disapproval?

These communication hiccups can be major headaches, especially when important things are at stake! Luckily, Media Richness Theory can help us navigate these muddy waters.

Media Richness to the Rescue

Remember our scale from Chapter 1? Richer communication, like talking in-person or on a video call, is a fantastic way to squash confusion. Here's why:

- **Ask and Answer:** Uncertainty is scary because you don't know what you don't know! Rich communication offers instant feedback. You ask questions, get clarification immediately, and fill in the missing information gaps.
- **Decoding the Unspoken:** When multiple meanings are possible (equivocality), seeing the person's face and hearing their tone of voice can be a lifesaver. A sarcastic text can be instantly understood as playful when you actually hear the person speak with a smile.
- **Adapting on the Fly:** Richness is flexible. When you see confusion on someone's face, you can change your explanation, offer an example, or draw a picture. It's much harder to do that with a text or email.

Real World Examples

- **The Misunderstood Memo:** Imagine a company-wide email with vague language about changes to a project. That's a recipe for uncertainty and equivocality! A short video call where people can ask questions would bring much more clarity.
- **The Relationship Text Trap:** You send your partner a simple "Okay" text after a disagreement. Did you mean, "Okay, I get it," or is it a passive-aggressive

"Okay, whatever"? A phone call would easily clear the air!

The Key Takeaway

When things are simple, leaner communication like email might be fine. But when stuff gets complicated, confusing, or leaves room for misinterpretation, richer is the way to go! Choosing the right communication tool can save you a ton of frustration and misunderstandings.

Chapter 3: Media Richness on the Job

Imagine your workplace as a giant communication highway. Emails zoom back and forth, quick messages fly in group chats, and you might even (gasp!) have an in-person meeting or two. But is all this communication actually getting you where you need to go? Media Richness Theory can be your road map to smooth operations at work.

MRT and Teamwork

Think of a group project. Would you tackle a big, complicated challenge by only sending emails? Probably not! MRT tells us that richer communication (video meetings, brainstorming in-person) works best when:

- **Solving Problems:** When something goes wrong, every detail matters. Hopping on a quick video call lets you share screens, see confused expressions, and quickly work toward a solution.
- **Building Relationships:** Teamwork is about more than just tasks. That hallway chat or grabbing coffee

together has a bonding power that a flurry of emails simply doesn't.

- **Sparking Creativity:** Sometimes the best ideas come from spontaneous conversations. Richer communication lets those "light-bulb moments" happen more naturally.

MRT and Leadership

Good leaders know that communication is key. Here's where MRT can make a difference:

- **Tackling Tough Topics:** Delivering bad news or providing critical feedback? Don't hide behind email! Richer communication lets you show empathy and address concerns head-on.
- **Big Announcements:** Company changes or new projects deserve more than a mass email. A video presentation or townhall meeting lets people see your commitment and ask questions.
- **Building Trust:** People trust you more when they can put a face to a name and see your sincerity. Regular rich communication builds stronger leader-team relationships.

Company Case Studies

- **The Email Avalanche:** One company relied too heavily on email for everything, leading to massive confusion and missed deadlines. Switching to video calls for complex discussions and weekly in-person check-ins turned things around!

- **The Remote Team Win:** A company with employees all over the world struggled with miscommunication. Implementing regular video calls, even for quick updates, made everyone feel more connected and productive.

MRT Best Practices

- **Routine Stuff:** Simple scheduling or updates? Lean communication like email is perfect.
- **Anything Tricky:** Complex problems, sensitive topics, or potential for misunderstanding? Go for richer communication.
- **Build Relationships:** Don't neglect the social side! Those informal "water-cooler" moments matter, even virtually.

Remember, choosing the right communication tool is like a skilled mechanic picking the right wrench for the job. Use MRT to make your workplace communication work for you, not against you!

Chapter 4: Media Richness Matters to the Heart

Think back to the last time you had a deeply meaningful conversation with someone you care about. Chances are, it wasn't over text message, right? Media Richness Theory helps us understand why the way we communicate has a huge impact on our closest relationships.

MRT and the Social Web

Staying connected is easier than ever – a quick social media post, a funny meme, a fire emoji. These are great, but MRT reminds us they're the "light snacks" of communication. Here's what we can miss out on with too much lean digital connection:

- **The Nuances of Emotion:** Sure, emojis help a bit, but they're no substitute for seeing a friend's smile or hearing the concern in their voice. It's those little cues that add depth to relationships.
- **True Understanding:** Sometimes you need a real back-and-forth talk to work through something

together. Text chains can leave too much room for misinterpretation and frustration.
- **Building Deep Bonds:** Sharing experiences in-person creates memories that last. There's a magic to shared laughter or witnessing a beautiful sunset together that a digital "like" just can't capture.

MRT and Romance

Love in the age of smartphones gets...complicated! Here's where MRT comes in:

- **Flirting and First Impressions:** Lean communication is okay for playful banter, but that first date? It deserves the richness of seeing each other's reactions in real time.
- "Are We Okay?": Dealing with conflict over text is a recipe for disaster. Those tough talks are often best handled face-to-face or at least with voice and tone to avoid hurt feelings.
- **Saying "I Love You":** Big heartfelt moments deserve the richest communication possible. Nothing quite beats expressing deep emotions in person.

MRT and Family Ties

Staying close with family can be tough, especially with busy schedules or living far apart. MRT shows us how to bridge the distance:

- **Checking In With Aging Parents:** Email is fine for updates, but regular video calls let you really see how they're doing and offer better emotional support.

- **The Bedtime Story Dilemma:** Reading to a child over video chat is better than nothing! But nothing beats snuggling up together with a book for true bonding time.
- **Big Family News:** Announcing a pregnancy or sharing tough stuff deserves richness. Don't let those precious moments happen over a group text.

The Key Takeaway

MRT doesn't mean ditching social media or never sending a text. It's about being mindful! When emotional closeness, avoiding hurt feelings, and truly understanding each other are important, go for the richest communication possible.

Chapter 5: The Future is...Virtual?

Buckle up, because we're about to blast off into the future of communication! Technologies like virtual reality (VR), augmented reality (AR), and even artificial intelligence (AI) are completely changing how we might connect in the years to come. This is where Media Richness Theory gets really interesting—and a little bit tricky.

Virtual Worlds, Real Feelings?

Imagine slipping on a VR headset and meeting up with your long-distance best friend in a digital coffee shop. You can see their gestures, hear their laughter, and almost feel like you're right there with them. Or a work meeting where AR overlays information onto the real world, making complex projects easier to visualize together. This is some next-level communication!

MRT has to evolve with these changes. Here's what we need to figure out:

- **The Emotion Factor:** Can a virtual hug ever truly replace a real one? Scientists are working to make digital experiences more emotionally rich, but will it ever feel completely the same?
- **Beyond Sight and Sound:** Maybe future tech will let us transmit smells, touch sensations, or even emotions digitally. That would add a whole new layer to the idea of media richness!
- **Making AI Personal:** Could you build a real friendship with a super-advanced AI chatbot? If it perfectly understands your words and responds emotionally, does that change the rules of MRT?

Worries and Wonders

Like with any cool new technology, there are both exciting possibilities and things to be cautious about:

- **The Loneliness Cure?** Could VR experiences help isolated people feel connected or provide realistic practice for difficult social situations?
- **Digital Divide:** Will everyone have equal access to these advanced communication tools, or will it create a gap between the tech haves and have-nots?
- **Too Much of a Good Thing?** Is it possible to get so immersed in the digital world that we neglect real-life relationships?

The Takeaway

The world of communication is wilder than ever before. Media Richness Theory gives us a way to think critically about these new technologies. It's a reminder that while fancy tools are awesome, it's the human connection that truly matters, whether it's in the real world or a digital one.

Chapter 6: MRT: Good Idea, but Not Perfect

Media Richness Theory is a powerful tool for understanding communication, but like any tool, it has its limits. It's important to remember that it's not a one-size-fits-all solution. Let's look at where MRT might fall short and explore some other ways to think about communication.

Where MRT Might Miss the Mark

- **We're All Different:** What feels like "rich" communication to one person might seem overwhelming to another. Some people thrive on video calls, while others get flustered and prefer the careful thought they can put into an email.
- **Culture Matters:** A thumbs-up emoji means one thing in the U.S. but might be rude in other cultures. MRT doesn't always account for how differently people around the world interpret cues and communication styles.

- **The Emotion Factor:** Sometimes a simple, heartfelt text can deliver more emotional impact than a stilted video call. MRT is focused on features of communication, but sometimes the intention behind the message matters more.
- **Beyond Words:** Think about two people who have inside jokes or a shared history. They might find deep meaning in a simple text that an outsider would find totally confusing. MRT doesn't fully capture this sort of special connection.

Other Ways to Think About Communication

MRT isn't the only game in town! Here are a few other interesting viewpoints:

- **Social Presence Theory:** This focuses on how connected you feel to the other person. Even a well-crafted text chain can build a strong sense of social presence if you're joking and sharing personal details.
- **Channel Expansion Theory:** This says that over time, you can make even a "lean" communication channel feel richer as you build a relationship with someone. Think about how those early awkward emails with a new coworker eventually become more relaxed and friendly.
- **Situational Factors:** Sometimes, you just don't have a choice! A noisy airport isn't ideal for a deep phone call. Other theories acknowledge that stuff outside of our control can majorly impact how well we communicate.

The Key Takeaway

Media Richness Theory is a valuable starting point. It helps us be more aware of our communication choices and their consequences. But to be truly great communicators, we need to also consider individual personality, cultural backgrounds, and the sometimes unpredictable situations life throws our way!

Chapter 7: Media Richness Reimagined

Get ready, because Media Richness Theory is about to get a serious upgrade! As technology evolves at breakneck speed, MRT has to keep up. Imagine a future where the ways we communicate feel almost like magic compared to what we have today.

MRT in a Sci-Fi World

Picture this:

- **Feeling the Feedback:** Gloves that let you "feel" a digital handshake or a pat on the back during a video meeting. This adds a whole new sensory layer to richness!
- **Emotion Translators:** Imagine software that analyzes your voice and facial expressions in real-time, helping you avoid misunderstandings even with people from very different backgrounds.
- **Brain-to-Brain Brainstorming:** Farfetched, yes, but what if we could directly share ideas and images

mentally? The ultimate in rich, unfiltered communication!

MRT in the Hybrid Workplace

The lines between work, home, and "on-the-go" are getting seriously blurred. MRT needs to evolve to help us navigate this complex environment:

- **Mixed-Reality Meetings** Could some people join a meeting in VR while others call in, all experiencing a similarly rich interaction? The tech challenges are huge, but so is the potential payoff.
- **The "Quick Question" Dilemma:** Is it okay to send a voice message to a coworker instead of typing? New communication norms will be needed so we don't drive each other crazy!
- **Combating Digital Burnout** With constant access to rich communication, how do we set boundaries and avoid overload? This is where mindfulness will be just as important as tech tools.

Where Do We Go From Here?

Researchers have their work cut out for them! Here are some exciting questions MRT needs to tackle:

- **Measuring the New Richness:** How do we assess communication when it involves senses beyond just sight and sound? We'll need new ways to evaluate what works best.

- **Ethics and Equity:** If some have access to ultra-rich communication tech and others don't, how do we ensure everyone can connect meaningfully?
- **The AI Factor:** Could we befriend AIs that flawlessly understand our feelings and intent? How will this redefine what it means to communicate effectively?

The Takeaway

The future of communication is thrilling and a little bit scary. Media Richness Theory, even as it evolves, gives us a framework to ask smart questions and make sure that our amazing new communication abilities bring us closer together, not further apart.

Conclusion: The Power of Mindful Connection

Throughout this book, we've journeyed into the world of Media Richness Theory (MRT). We've learned that the ways we communicate – from those quick text messages to face-to-face conversations – have way more impact on our lives than we might realize.

Key Takeaways to Remember

- **It's Not One-Size-Fits-All:** The right way to communicate depends on the situation. Sometimes a simple email is perfect; other times, you need the richness of a voice call or even meeting in person.
- **Uncertainty's Enemy:** Richer communication helps us squash misunderstandings and work through complex problems with better results.
- **Relationships Run on Richness:** Whether it's with friends, family, or romantic partners, truly connecting often means choosing communication methods that let you see and hear each other.

- **Technology is Tricky:** New technologies offer amazing possibilities, but they can also lead to confusion and even isolation. MRT helps us navigate this ever-changing landscape.
- **Think Before You Communicate:** MRT isn't about always using the fanciest tech. It's about being intentional, picking the tool that will get the best possible outcome.

Mastering Media Literacy

In a world overflowing with beeping smartphones, endless video calls, and social media overload, the ability to communicate wisely is more important than ever. Think of it like a superpower! Media literacy means:

- Understanding how different communication channels shape your message.
- Being adaptable and choosing the best way to connect for each situation.
- Using technology to build relationships, not replace them.

A Final Word

Media Richness Theory isn't a magic solution for perfect communication, but it's a start! By taking the time to learn about MRT, you've already set yourself apart. Keep this knowledge with you as you navigate work, relationships, and the increasingly digital world. Remember, it's not just what you say, but how you say it that truly matters.

About Freudian Trips

Welcome to Freudian Trips, your dedicated platform for diving deep into the world of psychology. We are more than just a YouTube channel or a book publisher. We are a beacon of enlightenment, making complex psychological concepts accessible and engaging for all.

Our YouTube channel is a rich repository of psychology made simple. We take the profound and often complex ideas from the world of psychology and break them down into digestible, easy-to-understand content. From the foundational theories of Freud to the cognitive insights of Piaget, we cover a broad spectrum of psychological schools and thoughts, making psychology accessible to everyone, regardless of their background or prior knowledge.

As a book publisher, we take the same approach, transforming intricate psychological theories into comprehensible narratives. Our books are not just collections of words, but vessels of wisdom that make psychology approachable and relatable. We believe that psychology should not be confined to academic circles, but should be available to all who seek to understand the human mind and behavior.

At Freudian Trips, we believe in the power of curiosity and the pursuit of knowledge. We are here to stoke the fires of your curiosity, to guide you on your intellectual journey, and to help you navigate the fascinating world of psychology.

If you are someone who is not afraid to question, to explore, and to learn, then you are in the right place. Join us on this journey of exploration, as we make psychology easy to understand, one concept at a time.

Be sure to visit our Youtube channel at: www.freudiantrips.com/youtube

You can also visit us on the web at www.freudiantrips.com

Welcome to The Freudian Trip community. Stay curious. Stay enlightened.